HOW TO GO
WASTE FREE

ECO TIPS FOR BUSY PEOPLE

CAROLINE JONES

D1473874

WELBECK

Published in 2019 by Welbeck
An imprint of the Welbeck Publishing Group
20 Mortimer Street
London W1T 3JW

Text © Welbeck 2019
Design © Welbeck 2019

All rights reserved. This book is sold subject to the condition that it may not be reproduced,
stored in a retrieval system or transmitted in any form or by any means, electronic,
mechanical, photocopying, recording or otherwise without the publisher's prior consent.

A catalogue for this book is available from the British Library.

ISBN 978-1-78739-347-9

Printed in China

10 9 8 7 6 5 4 3 2 1

CONTENTS

INTRODUCTION

Our beautiful planet has reached a crisis point. Decades of over-consumption, pollution and a cavalier attitude to waste disposal have wreaked havoc with our rivers, forests and oceans – we're literally drowning in an ever-increasing sea of rubbish.

Every year, humankind dumps over 1.8 billion tons (2 billion US tons) of waste worldwide. In the UK alone, an enormous 219.4 million tons (245.7 US tons) of household waste was produced in 2016. More worrying still, only 102.4 million tons (114.6 million US tons) of this was recycled, which means that more than half of all waste ended up polluting our planet to some degree.

About 50 per cent of unrecycled waste ends up buried in landfill sites, where some of it – but by no means all – will eventually rot and, in the process, generate methane gas, which contributes to global warming.

The rest ends up incinerated, which is not a good solution either, because plastics tend to produce toxic substances, such as dioxins, when they are burned. Gases from incineration have been linked to air pollution and also contribute to acid rain, while the ash created can contain heavy metals and other toxins that poison our soil.

And the rubbish that does not become landfill ends up as litter, dirtying our streets and slowly making its way into our rivers and oceans. Plastic pollution is killing our marine life – more than 7.8 million tons (8.8 million US tons) of plastic end up in our oceans each year, where
it can trap, entangle and poison the creatures that live there.

While leadership from global governments is needed to tackle this crisis, ignorance about the impact of our personal waste habits is also no longer an option. More and more research reveals that we will all need to change to reverse the devastating effects of plastic and other waste pollution on the environment and the wildlife in it.

So what can we do, as individuals, to stem this tide of trash? The good news is, the collective appetite for change has never been stronger. In London in 2019, the carefully planned 10-day Extinction Rebellion climate breakdown protest brought parts of the capital to a standstill – putting the urgency of environmental issues firmly in the headlines. Around the world, children inspired by Greta Thunberg take part in weekly school strikes, demanding action.

The message to every one of us is clear – we have to act now to protect our world for ourselves and for future generations.

One way we can all contribute is to reduce our personal waste footprint radically. Separating rubbish for recycling and using a bag-for-life for supermarket shopping may make you feel better, but it isn't nearly radical enough given the change that is needed. We should all be aiming for the goal of zero waste – or as near to it as humanly possible.

The zero-waste movement encourages individuals to produce absolutely no waste that can't be reused or composted – with even many recyclable products being avoided if possible. The simple goal of the movement is to keep all matter out of landfills. Make no mistake, moving towards a zero-waste lifestyle involves some serious changes in habit. Any reduction in domestic rubbish means rethinking the types of products we buy, as well as how we consume and dispose of them.

Peek inside your current household bin at the end of any week, and the thought of a zero-waste life can feel overwhelming – even impossible.

And yet, as with any radical, lasting change, going zero or very low waste starts by taking small steps. And once you get started on your rubbish-reduction journey, you'll quickly find your lifestyle will not only become more ethical and affordable, you'll also get rid of a lot of unnecessary stress and begin to reap the benefits of a simpler, healthier life.

Of course, a true low-waste lifestyle doesn't happen overnight, and it's easy to become paralyzed by all of the changes you could potentially make towards that goal. Which is where this book comes in.

How to Go Waste Free is designed as an easy guide to getting your own personal rubbish-reduction mission started. It's full of practical, and practically painless tips to help you chuck excess waste out of your life once and for all, bit by bit.

You'll find a host of simple ways to reduce the rubbish you produce in all areas of your life, one day at a time, whatever your budget, as you make the gradual transition from living a high-waste life to a low- or no-waste one.

From waste-free food shopping to learning how to compost and reducing your fast-fashion habit, this guide contains easy hacks and tricks to living more ethically. Think of it as the ultimate beginner's guide to joining the zero-waste revolution.

And in case you think that one person using less waste isn't going to save the planet, remember, this is how all positive change begins. We also have enormous collective power through the choices we make as consumers. Together, we can create demand for less wasteful ways to live and shop.

Inside these pages you'll find 100 tips that, taken together, would certainly lead to waste-free living – but you don't have to do them all at once. Just making one change a week, or even every fortnight, will eventually add up to a big difference, if you keep the momentum going month after month. Pick some easy product swaps first to motivate yourself, or maybe focus on the ideas that you believe could make the biggest impact on your lifestyle.

One great thing about making changes to help the environment is that these changes also make you feel good about yourself – and this feeling can become quite addictive, encouraging you to keep going and make bigger, bolder lifestyle changes as time goes on.

Plus this sort of positive change can be pretty contagious too, which means as soon as you've made an individual commitment to creating less waste, you'll boost the impact of your own choices just by chatting to family and friends about what you are doing and why. By explaining your personal decision to live a less wasteful life, you'll be inspiring others, who in turn can share their mission with even more people. Before too long a snowball effect will occur, creating a landslide of change in community after community – an eco revolution that really can help turn our world into a cleaner, less polluted place to live. Together we can make a difference.

GETTING STARTED

We all know we throw away too much waste, but in practice reducing it can be tough at first. The key is to begin gradually, sticking with a few simple changes until they become just a normal part of your day. Read on for how to begin your journey to a less wasteful life.

#1
MAKE NEW HABITS STCK

Living a low-waste lifestyle will ultimately require some significant changes to your daily routines – everything from how you cook dinner to cleaning the bathroom. Psychological studies show that in order to make any new change stick, it needs to become a habit. Habits form whenever we repeat a new behaviour enough times to imprint it on the brain – with estimates on the magic number of repetitions ranging from 28 to 50 times.

For daily behaviours, this translates to roughly four to seven weeks of change before choices that were initially conscious start to become automatic, and part of your daily routine for the long term.

#2
BREAK WITH THE OLD

Chucking stuff away without thinking is a lifelong habit for most of us – and one entrenched by years of repetition. It can make us feel tidy and more organized! Your first goal therefore is to break this old habit and replace it with a new behaviour of stopping and thinking every time you're faced with a waste-related choice. This might be as simple as, "Can I find another use for this or recycle it rather than just throw it away?" Or it could be a more radical decision such as, "Do I want to invest in a home composter instead of throwing all my food waste out?"

#3

AVOID ALL-OR-NOTHING THINKING

If you've ever tried to start a diet, you'll know that going into any new regime with a too strict mentality is a surefire route to failure. And just like cutting all carbs or only consuming juices is too difficult for most people to stick with, going from high to zero waste overnight isn't realistically achievable.

Outright bans set you up for failure. They're too difficult to maintain, which means your new low-waste habits won't have enough time to become embedded in your routine, and there's a high risk you'll simply revert to your old "just bin it" attitude because zero waste feels too hard.

So don't try to do it all in one go. Lasting success means taking it slowly, one step at a time, and making changes you can really live with. Some of the quick waste-free wins on the coming pages will help you start to create a new, greener mindset.

#4
DO A WASTE AUDIT

First things first, you need to work out just how much waste you are actually producing. An average person in the US produces about 1.9 kg (4.4 lb) of rubbish a day, while in the UK it's 1.4 kg (3 lb) – that's your own body weight in trash, every seven weeks. Do you produce more or less than this?

To find out means monitoring the quantity of rubbish in your life and identifying the areas where you most need to cut down – whether that's food, clothes, beauty products, paper or plastic packaging, or all of the above!

To get the ball rolling – starting on the day after your bins are collected – keep a waste diary for a week, monitoring how much rubbish your household throws away.

You can also put all your waste in a large bin bag and weigh it, and do the same with your recycling. If you make a note of those figures here, you can repeat this process after a month of rubbish reduction to see what progress you have made.

- **WEEKLY HOUSEHOLD WASTE IN KG (LB):**
- **WEEKLY RECYCLING IN KG (LB):**

#5
GET DOWN AND DIRTY WITH THE DETAIL

The next step is a bit yucky, but necessary if you really want to face up to just what you're actually throwing out – and to highlight which items are the worst offenders in your trash. Wearing rubber gloves, sift through everything in your bin and write down exactly what's there, using the chart below to guide you. You may be shocked at how much stuff you chuck away, but this should help spur you into action!

As you assess your weekly waste output, break it into categories. Write everything down in the following sections, listing how much of each item is there. For example, 3 plastic envelopes, 2 empty plastic milk bottles, 5 glass jars.

#6

GENERAL HOUSEHOLD WASTE

Food packaging ....

....

Food waste
(scraps and unwanted/out-of-date food) ....

....

Bathroom
(product bottles, old mascara tubes, cotton wool, etc.)...........

....

Other packaging
(unrecyclable envelopes, bubble wrap, etc.).......................

....

All other waste
(broken pens, used kitchen roll, batteries, etc.) ....

....

RECYCLING

Paper/cardboard ....

....

Plastic..

....

Glass ....

....

Metal...

....

#7
WORK OUT YOUR PRIORITIES

Seeing your waste habits starkly summarized in black and white will help you quickly identify the key areas you need to tackle first.

For example, are you creating a lot of rubbish by buying a coffee to go or a smoothie every day? If so, a great first step for you would be either to make coffee or smoothies at home and carry them to work in a reusable mug or flask, or to take your own container to your local coffee shop and ask them to fill it for you instead of using their takeaway cups. Many coffee places now offer you a discount for doing this because it saves them money too.

Or perhaps you're throwing away a lot more food than you realize. This means focusing on better meal planning and more regular shopping to reduce waste. It may also mean getting serious about composting (see page 72–3 for how to get started).

Or perhaps you're keen on beauty products and find yourself throwing away lots of empty bottles. Can you make changes here? For instance, trading cotton wool balls for a decent face cloth.

At first, coming face to face with all the waste in your life can feel overwhelming, but once you break down the causes into different areas and systematically focus on one at a time, making changes seems much less daunting.

#8
REMEMBER THE 5 RS

In 2012 zero-waste pioneer and blogger Bea Johnson came up with the "5 Rs" as the key things to remember when it comes to achieving a waste-free lifestyle. Apply them to your household waste list on page 15 and see which you can action, then commit the 5 Rs to memory.

The 5 Rs

Refuse
Say no to plastic-wrapped fresh produce and learn to turn down freebies. Refuse to buy cheap, unsustainable products that cost more in the long run.

Reduce
Do you really need another pair of jeans, a lipstick or that bottled drink? Free yourself from the trap of buying stuff to boost your mood.

Reuse
Rather than throwing an item away, find a way to reuse, repair or upcycle it. This goes for everything from jars to clothes and furniture.

Recycle
Recycle absolutely every scrap of packaging you can. When it comes to clothes, furniture or other items of value, donate them to charity.

Rot
Compost all food scraps – they won't break down in landfill for decades because of the lack of light and oxygen.

#9
THINK BIGGER PICTURE

As well as reducing the waste you create on a personal level, there are plenty of ways to get involved in campaigning to help make a difference on a larger scale. See if any local schools, cafés or businesses are keen to embrace zero waste – and if you can help them in their attempts to go about it.

Organizations such as Greenpeace and Friends of the Earth are also a good place to start, as is the Love Food Hate Waste campaign. It's also worth checking out bloggers such as Kathryn Kellogg at goingzerowaste.com and Celia Ristow's litterless.com for more ideas.

#10
DRUM UP SUPPORT

The zero-waste movement is growing rapidly around the globe. So wherever you live, even in the smallest town, there will be other people in your local area who have committed to the same quest.

Check online for local waste-free living forums and Facebook groups based near you. They are a great place to swap ideas on reducing waste, tap into local initiatives and find out where food composters and other recycling points are. You'll also find it easier to keep up the momentum if you're in touch with fellow waste-reducers who can offer advice and swap stories, making you feel part of the larger, zero-waste community.

#11
DON'T GO ON A SPENDING SPREE!

The buzz of throwing yourself into a new lifestyle change can be intoxicating – especially one that has such huge benefits for the planet. But this doesn't mean rushing out and enthusiastically buying every zero-waste replacement items you can find in one spree.

Not only is this prohibitively expensive, but shopping-led solutions are not the ideal start for the reduced consumption vibe you're aiming for here. Plus, throwing a perfectly good item out just because it's not "green" is very wasteful in itself!

Instead, pace your lifestyle replacements properly, and buy zero-waste alternatives only once your current items run out.

#12
DON'T LOSE HEART

Going waste free won't happen overnight. It might even take a year or two to get to super-low waste levels, if that's your goal. But just wanting to make changes and create slightly less waste is an achievement in itself, and one worth celebrating.

And while it's good to get tips and inspiration from those online, try not to compare yourself to them. Everyone's waste-free journey is different and every reduction in rubbish worthwhile.

Cut waste to save cash!

As if helping to save the planet isn't incentive enough, going zero waste will ultimately save you a whole heap of money to boot.

Admittedly, with reusable items there is often an upfront cost, but investing in lasting solutions really does save money in the long run.

For example, if you replace high-waste kitchen items, such as cling film (Saran wrap) and kitchen towels, with a reusable alternative, such as beeswax wrap, it will take only weeks to pay for itself. Swapping a fast-fashion habit for good-quality clothing may take a little longer to pay back, but the right wardrobe staples can last for years.

Another good example of saving money while saving the environment is shaving choices. If you buy a reusable metal safety razor, it will be five or six times the cost of a disposable one, but the razor could last you years with new blades costing hardly anything every three to six months, so you will make your money back in no time.

For women, a menstrual cup costs more in the short term but lasts for a good 10 years. Compare this to the financial outlay every month on disposable sanitary products, and you'll have recouped your money in less than a year.

Reusable face flannels for cleansing your skin are also much cheaper over time than expensive face wipes or cotton wool.

Shopping secondhand for clothing, books and furniture, instead of buying brand new every time, can save heaps of money too.

You'll also find that bulk and loose refills of food items such as beer, wine, oils and dry goods are often cheaper than their pre-packaged equivalents – and you can just buy the exact amount you actually need, saving even more money.

Taking your own reusable cup will get you a discount at many coffee chains now, and carrying your own water bottle means you can get a free refill at many places.

Some of the savings are small and slow to pay back, but it all adds up, and you'll soon find that with an overall low-waste lifestyle, you'll be spending a lot less than you did before – guaranteed!

PUTTING ZERO WASTE INTO PRACTICE

FOOD

In a world where people still starve to death and thousands of families on low incomes in developed countries have to rely on food banks, good food shouldn't end up tossed out with the rubbish. Yet time after time it does – and nearly everyone is guilty. Recent figures from WRAP, the government-funded programme to encourage recycling, show that households in the UK throw away close to 6.9 million tons (7.8 million US tons) of food each year, while households in the US waste an incredible 33 million tons (36.9 million US tons) – much of which is perfectly edible.

And because we all bin so much unwanted produce, food waste is also perhaps the single biggest focus area for personal change if you are embarking on a zero-waste lifestyle. All of which means we need to sit back and think about why exactly we are throwing away so much food – and find better solutions for avoiding needless waste next time.

Food for thought

scary facts and figures to make you sit up and think

- With a total value of £15 billion ($19 billion), in the UK almost £70 ($90) of food per household is thrown away every month – or enough to fill 4,000 Olympic swimming pools!

- On average we dump eight meals per household every week, instead of using up the leftovers or freezing them.

- The equivalent of 120 million chickens end up being thrown away each year.

- Almost half of the food produced in the world ends up as waste.

- Fresh vegetables and salad top the waste league of shame, making up more than a quarter of food that gets tossed.

- Bread, milk, carrots, fruit juices, fizzy drinks, meat and fish are among the other top 10 items chucked out with other rubbish.

- In Europe and North America, the average waste per person is 95–115 kg (209–253 lb) per year, whereas in sub-Saharan Africa, south and south-east Asia, it's only 6–11 kg (13–24 lb) per person.

#13
DO A FOOD AUDIT

The first thing you need to get to grips with is how much food you – and the rest of your household – are chucking out. And after doing the bin audit in Chapter 1, you should now be an old hand at monitoring your waste! This time, write down every item of food you throw out, from the smallest carrot top to the largest piece of out-of-date meat.

The best way to do this is simply keep a notepad on the counter nearest your kitchen bin. Keep the diary for two full weeks, then look carefully over your list.

We're all creatures of habit, so there's a good chance you're repeatedly binning the same items, which will make it easier to adjust your habits accordingly. Leftover lasagne scraped into the bin every time? Can you start having it for lunch the next day? Or freeze it for a night you don't want to cook? Maybe it's as simple as reducing the amounts in your regular recipe or investing in a smaller baking tray.

Once you have an idea of what gets wasted on a regular basis, the first steps to solving it are your shopping habits. Try the following tips to stop you buying food you don't need in the first place.

#14
USE UP FOOD YOU HAVE NOW

While you are meal planning, remember to take a quick inventory of your refrigerator and cupboards to see what ingredients you don't need to buy. In fact, it's a good idea to try to base at least a couple of meals from early in the week on what you already have in hand. By starting your weekly meal plan with what's already in the refrigerator, you'll use things up before they spoil, and waste less.

#15
TAKE A SHELFIE BEFORE YOU SHOP

Overbuying accounts for a huge amount of household food waste. Just think about how often you purchase food you don't really need, or duplicate items you already have because you can't quite remember what's on your shelves. Simply photographing the contents of your refrigerator before you go to the shops could help reduce unnecessary doubling-up.

#16
MEAL PLAN LIKE A PRO

Planning meals is the perfect way to reduce food waste and save money, because carefully measured meals will help you buy only what you need to create each dish. Proper planning can be a bit time-consuming at first, but it will soon become a habit. Before your big weekly shop, simply write down a full seven days of meals, making a careful list of all the ingredients you'll need to buy.

#17
MAKE A PLAN FOR LEFTOVERS

As you choose what meals to make, think about which leftovers will make great building blocks for other meals that week. For example, if you roast a whole chicken, you can make stock with the carcass and chop up the leftover meat for use in soup, sandwiches or maybe even a spicy curry.

#18
CHOOSE "DOUBLE DUTY" MEALS

Cooking a dish you can eat again on a second night not only saves on waste, it also means a night off from cooking! For example, add some extra spice to a tasty vegetarian pasta sauce and you have the basis for a nice chilli with rice on a second night.

#19
MAKE A DETAILED SHOPPING LIST

Don't forget to turn your weekly meal planner into an itemized shopping list – with a focus on loose, fresh ingredients that comes without excess packaging. Amazingly, fully one third of people don't write shopping lists, according to research by WRAP, and it's a bad habit that leads directly to food waste. To form good food habits, keep a magnetic pad and pen on the refrigerator door and note down items as and when they run out.

#20
STOCK YOUR PANTRY

Takeout food guarantees packaging waste and more often than not creates food waste too. To avoid falling back on your go-to delivery when you're tired or in a hurry, you need to make sure there are some easy, quick-fix standby meals on hand.

A well-stocked pantry is the secret to turning odd bits of food left in the refrigerator into a tasty meal. Cupboard essentials that last a long time and can be used to create a speedy meal include dried pasta, rice, lentils, tinned tomatoes, tinned fish, tinned beans, chickpeas – plus all your favourite dried herbs and spices.

#21
TAKE REUSABLE BAGS

By now we all know about the environmental impact caused by plastic shopping bags. In fact, since each plastic bag takes around 1,000 years to break down, the damage lasts a lot longer than you might think. Most shops now charge shoppers for plastic bags in an attempt to encourage more people to bring their own – but there is still a long way to go before we eliminate single-use plastic bags completely.

The best way to make sure you are never caught without a bag-for-life is to invest in a convenient cloth bag. These pack down to almost nothing and can fit in any handbag or coat pocket. And if you do ever forget to bring your bags for life to the supermarket, turn around and go and get them – after having to do this once, you won't forget again!

#22
SHOP LOCALLY

Buying smaller amounts of fresh produce more regularly from local shops means you get the chance to use up every item before it goes off. By shopping local you'll also inject more cash into your community and help keep smaller, independent shops in the area, improving the chances that more people will shop locally and help reduce food waste. A short walk to the local shops is also good daily exercise – much better for you than just waiting for the internet shopping to arrive!

#23
BUY ONLY WHAT YOU NEED

Don't be afraid to buy small, specific amounts – if a recipe calls for two carrots, there's no pressure to buy a whole bag. Instead, buy loose produce so you can purchase the exact number you'll use in the next few days. You can always return to the shops for more produce later. Likewise, try buying grains, nuts and spices from bulk bins in larger stores or healthy food shops, so that you can measure out exactly what you need and won't overbuy, or overspend!

#24
HAVE A "CAN DO" APPROACH

Canned and frozen fruits and vegetables are a good solution if you aren't sure you'll be able to use up fresh foods before they go off. They are often more affordable than fresh varieties and can even be more nutritious because they are canned just hours after being picked, which helps retain most of their vitamins.

#25
BE HONEST ABOUT YOUR NEEDS (AND HABITS)

You may have good, healthy eating intentions but if you live alone, it's unlikely you'll ever consume a bumper-sized bag of apples. So don't be tempted to buy them, even if the larger serving sizes seem to offer better value. And if you know you rarely cook, don't stock up on lots of ingredients that have to be cooked before you can eat them – chances are, they will go off before you're tempted to head into the kitchen.

#26
BUY QUIRKY SHAPES

Many fruit and veg are thrown away because their size, shape, or colour isn't in line with the way most supermarket shoppers think these items should look. But this produce is still perfectly good to eat and will taste the same. Seeking out these imperfect items from the local farmer's market or grocery store will help use up food that might otherwise be thrown away. Some supermarkets have now started offering odd-shaped fruit and veg too.

#27
STOP BUYING FIZZY WATER

If you love sparkling water, but not the single-use plastic it comes in, invest in a home carbonation machine, and you'll be cutting down on a large source of single-use plastic. A million plastic bottles are bought around the world every minute, and fewer than half those bought in 2016 were collected for recycling. Instead most plastic bottles produced will end up in landfill or in the ocean.

Some models come with a glass rather than plastic bottle and can turn tap water into a bubble-filled drink in seconds. The machines do represent an upfront investment but they will also save you money in the long run. Gas canisters for a carbonator are very affordable and make 60 litres (13 gallons) of sparkling water, whereas the same volume of sparkling bottled water from a leading brand will cost you nearly three times as much.

#28
GET TO KNOW YOUR MILKMAN

Supermarket milk comes in plastic bottles which, while recyclable in theory, require more energy to be made, and only 75 per cent are fully recycled – some 25 per cent end up in landfill or the ocean. Your greenest bet is to go old school and start using a local milkman because each glass bottle is reused on average 15 times, sometimes as many as 50, before being recycled. Visit findmeamilkman.net to find one in your area if you're in the UK, or search online for "local milk delivery" to find one of the many delivery services available around the world. Many organic food box providers will also deliver dairy products.

#29
FOLLOW FIFO WHEN UNPACKING

When you're unpacking shopping, stick to the "first in, first out" rule, organizing items by the use-by dates, moving new products to the back of cupboards and refrigerators. This way, you're more likely to use up the older stuff before it expires, instead of simply forgetting about it.

#30
SEPARATE FAST-SPOILING VEG

When it comes to fruit and veg, storing fast-ripening types separately can be the key to ensuring a longer shelf life for all. The problem is, fruit and veg that ripen fast also produce gases during ripening, which quicken the ripening process of their neighbours in the fruit bowl or veggie drawer and make them spoil faster too.

For example, although both apples and watermelons like being stored in the refrigerator, apples produce high levels of ethylene, which can turn watermelons mushy. And bananas should always be kept on their own, as this famously fast-ripening soft fruit also produces potent enthylene gas that will result in most fruit or veg ripening too quickly and spoiling. Lastly, if you don't want to throw away potatoes, make sure you don't store them near any onions, as onions produce a small amount of ethylene gas that can taint potatoes with an unwelcome, pungent flavour.

#31
USE YOUR LOAF

We throw away shocking amounts of unused bread, often due to bad storage decisions. For a longer-lasting loaf, keep it in a cool, dark place but never the refrigerator, where it can lose moisture and become stale very quickly. You can also freeze bread for longer-term storage. For instance, if you find you're often throwing half a sliced loaf away, freeze half when you first buy to keep it fresher, and defrost slices in a toaster as needed.

#32
LEARN ABOUT LABELS

Understanding the "use by" and "best before" dates of food is also key to cutting waste. The "use by" date is about safety and the most important date to remember. Foods can be eaten – and most can be frozen – up until the "use by" date, but not after.

The "best before" date refers to the quality and taste. The food will be safe to eat after this date but may not be at its very best in terms of flavour and texture. "Best before" can be a useful guide, but when push comes to shove, you can't beat looking, smelling and tasting for a reliable indicator of freshness.

WASTE-PROOF YOUR REFRIGERATOR

Simply storing food correctly in the fridge can be a huge boost to reducing food waste. Here are the dos and don'ts you need to know to get the best shelf-life out of your refrigerated foods.

#33
CHILL OUT

According to the Love Food Hate Waste campaign, the average refrigerator temperature is too warm, at 7°C (45°F), when the ideal setting should be 5°C (41°F) or less. This might only be a couple of degrees difference, but maintaining your refrigerator at the right temperature could extend the life of milk, yoghurts and cooked meats by an extra three days, experts say, cutting food waste significantly. To find out how to reset your refrigerator to the correct temperature, take a look at the brand-by-brand "Chill The Fridge Out" temperature tool at lovefoodhatewaste.com

#34
PACK IT RIGHT

Store food in the correct place in the refrigerator. It's colder near the bottom and so that's where you should keep perishables such as meat and dairy. Another reason to keep meat on the bottom shelf of the refrigerator is this: here it has the lowest potential to drip and contaminate other items. And if you realize you won't be using it within two days, freeze it.

#35
REFRIGERATOR OR CUPBOARD?

Eggs are best kept in the refrigerator, but you can keep them fresher for longer by simply leaving them in the eggbox. Cucumbers and tomatoes, on the other hand, actually last longer when stored at room temperature – unless they've already been sliced, after which they should be kept in the refrigerator.

#36
BOTTLE IT

Glass jars and bowls with airtight lids should be your storage container of choice, as they will keep food as fresh as any non-recyclable plastic container. Glass can also withstand cold and even freezing temperatures, and is easy to clean, so it won't become unpleasantly stained like plastic containers. Plus, if you buy oven-proof toughened glass such as Pyrex, you can transfer dishes straight from the refrigerator to the oven and vice versa.

Glass, meanwhile, does not react with food or affect its flavour, and it doesn't warp in the microwave or dishwasher either.

If you're buying new, Kilner makes a great range of glass storage jars, but you should definitely consider reusing old jam, sauce and pickle jars. Simply wash them out thoroughly or run them through the dishwasher with your normal dishes.

#37
STEEL YOURSELF

Steel containers are another good option and, unlike plastic, won't stain or degrade in contact with acidic foods such as tomato sauces. Steel can also be washed safely at high temperatures. Plus the rectangular "tiffin box" variety are designed to stack neatly, making them great space-savers in the refrigerator. The only drawback is that you can't see what's inside – to get round this, use a wipeable pen to mark what's inside.

#38
BEE CLEVER

The best alternative to cling film (Saran wrap) and single-use plastic food bags is probably reusable beeswax wrap. It's made from cotton fabric soaked in beeswax and vegetable oil, and can be moulded around food or used to seal a food container. The wrap is highly reusable and just needs cleaning with cold, soapy water and laying out to dry. One wrap should last a year and then can be put on a compost heap. The only downside is, you can't wash it in hot water, which means they're fine for dry foods, but not for storing meat or fish in. They are widely available online, and you can also easily make your own.

#39
KEEP A LID ON IT

Another good option to cover foods are stretchy silicone lids, widely available at Amazon and eco shops, which can simply be pulled over dining bowls and other containers to form an airtight seal. Silicone is made from silica in sand and is not toxic to human and marine life. It is also more durable than plastic, can withstand hot and cold temperature fluctuations better and is completely recyclable after a lifetime of use.

#40
IT'S A WRAP

Forget supermarket plastic packing. Storing meat from your local
butcher or fish from the fishmonger in a parchment paper parcel,
followed by a layer of aluminium foil, is a greener option – especially
if you've taken your own eco container to collect the food in first. The
environmentally friendly brand If You Care has Forest Stewardship
Council-approved, unbleached and compostable parchment paper
and also makes recycled aluminium foil, which can be washed and
reused. Foil that is too crumpled to be reused can also be recycled
once wiped clean.

#41
KEEP FRUIT FRESH

The plastic wrap that fruit, vegetables and salad from the supermarket tends to come in can actually make these foods soggy and go mouldy sooner. Most fruit and veg will keep very well stored loose in your fridge's veg drawer, but to transport loose produce and keep items stored tidily, try using cotton mesh produce bags (found in eco shops or online). If you dampen the bags with a little water before you put them in the fridge, the moisture will keep veg crisper for longer. Soft fruit such as berries is better stored in glass.

COOKING

There are a whole host of clever tips that waste-conscious cooks can employ to become more frugal in the kitchen. Here are some ideas to get you started.

#42
COOK BASED ON FRESHNESS

Note upcoming expiration dates on foods you already have at home, and plan meals around the products that are closest to their expiration. On a similar note, keep a list of what's in the freezer and when each item was frozen. Post this list on the freezer door for easy reference, and use items before they pass their prime.

Reduce your meat consumption

A raft of research in recent years has laid bare the hefty impact that eating meat – especially red meats such as beef and pork – has on the environment, from fuelling climate change to polluting our rivers.

Despite dominating the vast majority of farmland, meat and dairy accounts for less than 20 per cent of all food calories eaten by humans, making it an incredibly inefficient method of food production. The truth is that any version of farmed meat, including organic, is a wasteful use of resources. For instance, it takes a shocking 17,000 litres (3,700 gallons) of water to make 1 kg (2.2 lb) of beef.

Add to this the deforestation needed to make way for livestock, which links meat-rearing practices to the extinction of other animals, and the role of livestock waste as a significant pollutant of our rivers and oceans.

Then there is the devastating effect on climate change to consider. It is estimated that greenhouse gases from farm cows and the use of fertilizer, measured as CO_2 equivalent, are greater than those from all the world's cars.

Many advocates believe our only hope to keep the global temperature increase from breaching the 2°C limit agreed by governments worldwide is if the developed world moves towards a more flexitarian diet – which means eating less meat, less often. Shifting to more plant-based foods is essential to combat climate change, soil, air and water pollution, ocean dead zones, and myriad other problems caused by industrial livestock production.

This is all without mentioning the huge impact of a meat-rich diet on human health, on which the research is equally clear. A diet heavy in meat increases our risk of obesity, cancer and heart disease. Add all this together, and you can start to see the true cost of that roast chicken or beef burger.

Indeed, a report on world diet compiled by a global commission of 37 experts from 11 countries, and published in respected medical journal *The Lancet* in 2019, concluded with a simple piece of advice: "Here's what to eat to save yourself and the planet: less meat and sugar, more fruits and vegetables."

#43
EAT LESS MEAT

Turning vegan overnight may not be an option for everyone, but if we all make a pledge to cut down on the number of weekly meals with meat or dairy, it will have a huge impact on both human health and the health of the planet. Here are some simple tips to get you started.

- If you have a big meat habit to kick, start small: try Meatless Mondays at first. Then build up to two or three days a week of vegetarian or even vegan eating, and eventually alternate days of meat and no meat, so you're halving your overall intake.

- Keep red meat to a once-a-week treat and eat more fish – ensuring that they are sustainable varieties that are not being overfished. Check on the Marine Conservation Society's Good Fish Guide website for details: **www.mcsuk.org**

- Seek out new proteins and form meals around them rather than meat. Tofu, lentils, beans, chickpeas, teff, quinoa, nuts and seeds are good alternatives.

- Make fresh fruits and veg a bigger part of your diet. Start by thinking of veg as the majority part of every meal, not just a side dish.

- Buy local, organic fresh produce whenever possible.

#44
BECOME A MORE CREATIVE CHEF

Using up what's in your refrigerator and revitalizing leftovers means closing the trusty cook book and being more creative. No mince for Bolognese sauce? No problem, make a healthier veggie version using lentils. No chickpeas to make hummus? Blend other beans such as butterbeans in their place. The following tips will give you even more ideas to inspire your own cooking improvisation.

#45
EAT UP THOSE LEFTOVERS

Lots of us keep leftovers only to throw them away unused two days later, which is just as wasteful as never having saved them in the first place! Get into the habit of actually eating evening meal leftovers for lunch the next day, or pop them into a Mason jar and take to work for a packed lunch. Most workplaces should provide a microwave for reheating food. If your office is currently without one, make sure to lobby your boss to get one! And if you don't want to eat leftovers the day after they're cooked, freeze and save them for later – then add this meal to your next weekly meal planner so you don't forget it.

#46
HAVE A WEEKLY "USE IT UP" MEAL

Designate one dinner each week to use up all the bits and pieces you've got left from your week's cooking. This means scouring the cupboards and refrigerator for leftovers and ingredients that might otherwise be overlooked and then dreaming up a dish that puts them all together. Buddha bowls are great for this – you can layer foods such as rice and pasta with sliced veg and other toppings, and serve with dips and breads for an eclectic but tasty meal.

#47
EKE OUT FLAVOUR

Often the by-products from cooking processes can be turned into something delicious in their own right. For example, you can make tasty stocks and soup bases from meat bones, veg peelings and citrus fruit. You can also use the rinds of hard cheeses to flavour sauces.

#48
JUICE IT

Fruit and veg don't have to be thrown away just because they've gone a little soft. Throw fruit into a smoothie, and wilting veg into soups. Or blend both to create tasty juices that are super healthy.

#49
THINK OF LEFTOVERS AS FILLINGS

Leftover chilli or curry not quite enough for a full meal? Why not use it as a filling for a delicious wrap, burrito or taco? Or maybe see it as a light snack to have with flat bread or tortilla chips.

#50
EMPLOY PORTION CONTROL

Avoid cooking (and wasting) too much pasta, rice and lentils by learning to stick to the recommended serving sizes listed on packaging, instead of judging amounts by eye. You can also pick up rice and pasta measurers pretty cheaply to eliminate the need to weigh food.

#51
REPURPOSE OLD BREAD

Bread rolls past their best? Put them in the oven for a few minutes to crisp up again. You can also make stale bread into breadcrumbs by blitzing it in a food processor, and they can be stored in the freezer to get out when you need them. Mix the crumbs with herbs and onions and you have a fabulous stuffing for chicken or peppers, or maybe use to sprinkle on baked fish for an extra-crunchy topping.

#52
GET SAUCY OR BE DIPPY

Lots of leftovers can be made into sauces or dips. If you've got any unused beans or pulses, you can mash or blend them with some garlic, lemon juice and herbs for a tasty dip. Slightly overripe avocados are great for guacamole, and tomatoes, peppers and cucumbers that need using up can be chopped into a homemade salsa.

#53
USE UP EXCESS FRUIT

Slice and combine fruits that are close to being past their best into a fruit salad, or use as a topping for porridge. Cook berries, apples or pears for a few minutes in a saucepan with one tablespoon of water to make a delicious compote, and use it to make a fruit crumble or a tasty yoghurt topper. Use overripe bananas in muffins, cakes and smoothies.

#54
DON'T CHUCK OLD VEG

Add any uneaten vegetables to soups, stews, casseroles, pasta sauces or omelettes. Or combine cold cooked veg with a little salad dressing or vinegar for a nutritious side dish or snack.

#55
EAT THE LOT

When cooking, try to use every piece of whatever veg you're prepping, instead of simply throwing away the ends and peel. For example, leave the skin on cucumbers and potatoes, sauté tasty and nutritious broccoli stems along with the florets, and clean rather than cut off carrot and parsnip tops before cooking. As well as cutting down on waste, the skin and stems offer lots of extra flavour, and often contain the highest concentration of nutrients, so you'll be boosting your vitamin intake and health at the same time.

Make friends with your freezer

- To the surprise of some, bread defrosts perfectly and can happily be stored in a freezer for up to six months. So always freeze any loaves that won't be used right away or even any leftover slices from a meal. All types of bread and rolls do, however, freeze better if you transfer them into a reusable, eco-cloth freezer bag rather than leave them in the packaging they came in.

- Recipe only require half an onion? Slice and chop it all, then freeze what you don't need in a small glass jar. You can toss the onion into a frying pan straight from frozen.

- Puree leftover chilli, garlic and ginger and freeze the mixtures in ice cube trays. Popping one or two "spice cubes" into curries and stir-fries will add instant flavour. The same goes for any fresh herbs like basil and coriander (cilantro) if they start going limp – simply chop and mix them with a little olive oil or butter and freeze in ice cube trays for later use in pasta dishes and soups.

- Leftover cooked veg that will otherwise go to waste? It will freeze perfectly fine for use later dropped into casseroles, soups or stir-fries.

- Chop soft fresh fruits and store in stainless steel tins in the freezer for use in smoothies, compotes and crumbles. This tin technique works best with berries.

- Don't forget that dairy freezes well too – simply transfer into a glass jar or bottle with a secure lid. Semi-skimmed and skimmed milk freezes better than whole milk, which can separate. But if your milk does separate once defrosted, a good shake should sort it. Hard cheese also freezes well – cut it into smaller portions, or grate some ready for use later.

- Freeze leftover wine in an ice cube tray. The frozen cubes can then easily be added into gravies, soups and stews for an added flavour boost.

#56
PICKLE OR BOTTLE IT

Both fruits and vegetables can be preserved through an easy pickling process. Alternatively, you could use them to create simple homemade jellies, jams or chutneys.

RECIPE 1
SPEEDY PICKLED VEG

You'll need:
125 ml (4½ fl oz) rice or apple cider vinegar
15 ml (1 tbsp) sugar
5 ml (2 tsp) sea salt
150 g (5 oz) thinly sliced vegetables, such as carrot,
    cauliflower, red onion and cucumber

To make:
Whisk the vinegar, sugar, and salt in a small bowl until they're completely dissolved. Then add vegetables and let sit for at least 10 minutes before serving.

RECIPE 2
EASY SOFT-SET JAM

You'll need:
900 g (2 lb) of any soft fruit, such as strawberries,
raspberries, hulled cherries
½ vanilla pod
200 g (7 oz) high pectin sugar (jam sugar)
60 ml (4 tbsp) lemon juice
2 x empty glass jars with lids
A cook's thermometer

To make:
Sterilize the jars and their lids by boiling for 10 minutes
in a water-filled saucepan or running them through your
dishwasher's hottest wash. Get a large saucepan, add all
the ingredients and mash them up together with a potato
masher or similar. Place on a low heat and stir until all the
sugar has dissolved. Increase the heat and bring to the boil,
stirring often, until it reaches 104–5°C (219–21°F) on the
thermometer. Carefully skim off any foam and let the mixture
cool a little. Finally, pour into the sterilized jars and seal tight
with lids. Allow to cool and keep in the refrigerator for use
within two to three weeks.

#57
SHARE SPARE FOOD

Got a glut of apples or bought too much bread? Ask your neighbours if they could make use of them – they won't be offended! Or you could always make sure it gets properly used by donating it to your local food bank – look online to find your nearest one.

There are also apps such as OLIO that connect you with both neighbours and local shops, so that any surplus food can be shared rather than thrown away. To give away an item, just add a photo and short description, and list when and where the item is available for pick-up.

#58
HAVE A CUPBOARD AMNESTY

Go through your pantry and be honest about those food items you'll never use, and box them up. Any canned food or dried goods that you know will still be sitting there in 12 months' time can be donated to local food banks or soup kitchens before they expire, which means they will be eaten by somebody who really needs them rather than going unused.

#59
EXPLORE OTHER OPTIONS

If there is absolutely no space for doing your own composting, see what other solutions there are available for you. Does your local council collect food waste each week, or is there a farm or local composting scheme in your area where you can take your scraps? Farms often accept organic waste which they can use for fertilizer, while newer composting schemes actually transform it into low-carbon electricity to help power homes.

#60
BECOME A MASTER COMPOSTER

If you're not currently recycling food waste for collection or composting it yourself, then most of the weight in your rubbish bin is probably coming from food scraps. Disposing of food waste with the normal rubbish collection means it ends up in landfill, where it can sit for many years. By home composting, you're seriously slashing the amount of rubbish you put out for collection and also creating a free and package-free fertilizer that will help everything in your garden grow.

Your first step to getting started with composting is identifying the system that will work for your home and what it will and won't digest.

- A standard composter will recycle raw food waste, including: vegetable peelings, fruit waste, teabags, coffee grounds, plant prunings and grass cuttings. Slower to break down but also compostable in a standard system are crushed eggshells, egg and cereal boxes, toilet and kitchen roll tubes, twigs, natural fibre cloth scraps, tissues, paper towels and shredded paper. However, a standard composter is not suitable for cooked veg, meat or dairy.

- A "hot composter" composts at self-generated temperatures of up to 60°C (140°F), which means the range of food waste that can be successfully added is much larger than with standard home composting. Hot composters have air valves and need regular aeration as well as frequent feeding with waste. A hot composter like the popular Green Johanna can recycle all the same food waste as the standard version, but you can also add all cooked foods, meat, dairy, bones – even old hair and finger nails!

- You can pick up most types of composters at local garden centres, or search online for a local organization that works with local councils to delive compost bins to your front door.

- Whatever type you choose, think big. Selecting the largest bin your outdoor space can accommodate offers a compost receptacle that tends to be much easier to use.

#61
STOP BUYING PLASTIC WATER BOTTLES

It's that simple. Single-use plastic has no place in a waste-free lifestyle, and the sadly ubiquitous water bottle is a good place to start. Don't leave your house without a full, reusable water bottle – the stainless steel variety has great green credentials, keeps water cool and doesn't have that horrible plastic smell.

Plus with more "water stations" popping up than ever before, it has never been easier to refill your reusable bottle with fresh water, which eliminates the need to buy a new one while out. Tap is an app that promotes the drinking of tap water and aims to reduce the use of bottled water. Enter your location on their app to find free "refilling stations" near you (find out more at www.findtap.com).

#62
INVEST IN A REUSABLE CUP

Bringing your own reusable cup to a local café for your daily brew is not only good for waste reduction – you'll avoid using a disposable plastic or paper cup – it could even save you money, as many coffee shops offer a discount for bringing your own receptacle. Good choices are those made from steel or natural bamboo fibre. Both are fully dishwasher-safe and have no plastic aftertaste, so your brew will taste better too.

#63
SIP WITH SUSTAINABLE STRAWS

A single plastic straw can take about 200 years to break down, yet an estimated 8.5 billion plastic straws are thrown away each year in the UK alone. The stark truth is this: even though straws are made from plastic that in theory can be recycled, they are too small to be regularly picked out during the separating process at recycling plants

Thankfully, more and more shops are swapping plastic straws for more environmentally friendly versions. Paper is a better choice because it is biodegradable, but bear in mind that paper straws come from trees and so contribute to deforestation, and most still end up in landfill. Your greenest bet is to buy and carry your own reusable metal or silicone straw with you. Or simply ask yourself honestly: "Do I really need a straw to consume drinks anyway?"

#64
PACK A WEEKDAY LUNCH...

...instead of eating out every day. Not only is a packed lunch more economical, it's a great way to use up leftovers and reduce your waste at home. Just pack food in stainless steel tiffin tins or glass jars. You'll also be bypassing the huge amount of waste involved in buying lunch to go from a coffee shop or salad bar – the (usually plastic) containers the food comes in, the disposable cutlery and the bag it's carried out in – all of which end up in the nearest bin half an hour later.

#65
DITCH DISPOSABLE PLATES AND CUTLERY

They may be handy for parties and picnics, but paper – or worse still, polystyrene – plates and cups create an enormous amount of waste because they're used just once and then tossed away. So even though it will mean more washing up, designate some cheaper dishes for picnic use.

Plastic cutlery is also chucked away after just one use, rarely recycled, and can take about 450 years to break down in landfill. Wooden cutlery is recyclable but depletes trees. So it's far more eco-friendly to invest in a reusable travel cutlery set, or just bring cutlery from home when you're planning to eat al fresco or grab a takeout.

#66
SAY NO TO FREEBIES

It almost goes without saying that the sort of food chains associated with free plastic toys for kids are not the kind of places anyone following a waste-free lifestyle should be frequenting. But if pester power wins out and you do find yourself making the odd trip to a big chain, always say no thank you to any promotional freebies on offer – the cheap plastic toys are rarely played with and just end up in your dustbin, then go straight to landfill.

#67
SPLIT FOOD WHEN OUT OR TAKE LEFTOVERS HOME

Research shows that food portions have increased by an incredible 25 per cent in the last 30 years, which can mean either consuming a huge number of excess calories – or wasting uneaten food. Don't be afraid to ask for a smaller portion when eating out, or why not split a main course or dessert with your partner or friend?

If sharing meals isn't your thing, just ask to take any leftovers home in a doggy bag. For bonus eco points, bring along your own reusable container! Then you'll have bagged yourself a ready-made free lunch for the following day.

WASTE-FREE
AROUND THE
HOME

Although the kitchen is undoubtedly the main room in which you can make the most obvious difference when it comes to leading a less wasteful home life, this doesn't mean there aren't plenty of other areas in your house that could easily become lower waste – and help you reduce your overall environmental damage footprint. From how you clean your home to the items you use in your bathroom and the clothes stored in your wardrobe, here are some ideas for spreading the waste-free vibe around the rest of your home.

CLEANING

Simplifying your home cleaning products from a raft of brightly coloured bottles to a few common, store-cupboard essentials will reduce your use of plastic, as well as the potentially harmful chemicals often used in shop-bought cleaners. Fewer chemicals also means less exposure to allergenic substances that could trigger skin reactions or worsen asthma.

Create a zero-waste cleaning kit

Ditch paper towels and other disposable cleaning items for good. Instead put together a handy kit with the following reusable basics, which should cover every cleaning need that crops up:

- A wooden scrubbing brush
- Metal scourer
- Feather duster
- An old toothbrush
- Dustpan and brush (made from metal or wood)
- Wooden broom
- A bag of reusable cloths – try making from old towels

#68
STEAM-CLEAN FLOORS

A steam mop is a pretty green way to clean floors because it only uses steam to clean and kill germs, and doesn't require any chemical detergents. It also comes with reusable mop heads, which you simply wash after each use.

Make your own green cleaning liquids

Recipe 1: Multi-Purpose Spray

To make:
Mix together half warm water and half white wine vinegar (which you can buy in glass bottles) in an old plastic spray bottle, or buy a stainless steel one.

To use:
This mixture can be used on most floors, bathroom and work surfaces, although it can dull marble and granite. If you do have those materials, it's best to test first on a small unseen area.

Recipe 2: Eco Bathroom Cleaner

To make:
Again, using a spray bottle, mix 200 ml (7 fl oz) of warm water with 1 tablespoon of liquid castile soap, such as Dr Bronner's. Add a couple of drops of lavender or peppermint essential oil if you'd also like it to smell good.

To use:
Spray directly to clean bathrooms and floors – or just about anything!

#69
BUY SOME BICARB

Bicarbonate of soda or baking soda can be used for so many different cleaning purposes, and can be bought and stored in recyclable cardboard boxes. It's also a powerful natural deodorizer, which is great for removing smells from refrigerators, carpets and upholstery.

For refrigerators, just leave a shallow bowl of bicarb on one of the shelves. For soft furnishings, sprinkle onto the area and leave for a few hours, then suck up using the small nozzle on your vacuum cleaner.

To clean your oven without chemicals or too much elbow grease, spray it with full strength vinegar, then sprinkle it with baking soda. Leave it overnight and in the morning, scrape the surfaces with a spatula, wiping everything clean with a damp cloth after.

BEAUTY AND GROOMING

Figures show that people in the UK – and the rest of the world too – do not recycle bathroom waste reliably. Perhaps it's simply that most bathrooms are upstairs from the main bin. Because, while up to 90 per cent of us recycle our kitchen waste, only half of us recycle bathroom products. On top of this, bathrooms are a place in which we often hoard a huge collection of plastic bottles, from shampoo to bath oil to face wash.

Indeed, the typical woman applies some 10–12 products in the morning before leaving the house – and that's without adding up all the other items stored in cabinets and under our sinks.

Thankfully, there are now plenty of low-waste alternatives for beauty lovers, from bamboo toothbrushes and shampoo bars to reusable face wipes. Here are some ideas to get you started.

#70
THINK MINIMALIST BEAUTY

Most of us use far more products than we actually need. As
well as creating excess waste and costing excessive amounts of money,
this is a surefire way to overcomplicate our morning and bedtime
routines. To kick things off, try removing 75 per cent of your daily
beauty products for a week, to help you separate the must-haves from
the non-essentials. It will soon become apparent which items or beauty
steps you need to add back in and which you can easily live without.
Donate any unwanted products to friends or family and embrace the
simpler life.

#71
SET A "ONE OUT, ONE IN" RULE

Make a commitment to only bring a new beauty product into the house when you've used up an old one. This will stop you accumulating unnecessary clutter and mean you finish what you already have before purchasing any eco beauty products – because it's possible to end up with more low-waste products than you need too!

#72
USE BAR SOAP INSTEAD OF LIQUID

Apart from the compostable paper they're wrapped in, bars are virtually waste-free – and when you've used them up there's nothing to throw away or recycle. Solid bars are super-concentrated too, so they last between three to six times longer than the bottled stuff. To go one better, ask yourself if you really need several separate soap bars for face washing, body washing and shampooing, or can you just use an all-in-one bar?

#73
FIND OTHER WAYS TO AVOID PLASTIC

When you're aiming for zero waste, even recyclable plastic is best avoided if possible. Thankfully you can buy a host of alternatives these days. Browse the shelves of your local health food or organic store, and you'll find bath oil stored in glass jars, hair conditioner in aluminium containers, even deodorant in compostable cardboard cylinders.

#74
TRY DRY SHAMPOO

It's a revelation! Not only can you buy dry shampoo in cardboard or metal containers, sprinkling a little on hair roots will absorb grease, boost volume and freshen hair. This can buy you an extra day of not washing hair, saving water and energy to boot.

Try making your own dry shampoo with this recipe.

You'll need:
120 g (4 oz) arrowroot or cornflour (cornstarch)
Optional: 2 tbsp cocoa powder if you have darker hair
4–5 drops of essential oil of your choice – lavender,
    rosemary or peppermint work well.

To make:
Mix all the ingredients together and keep in a glass jar.

To use:
Apply a light dusting with an old powder puff or make up
brush – using this will help ensure you don't put too much on,
which can make roots look dull and dusty.

Leave for 5 minutes to absorb excess oil, then brush roots
through thoroughly until none is visible.

#75
GET TOOTHPASTE IN A JAR

Traditional toothpaste comes in plastic tubes that are non-recyclable. Some eco fans happily just use baking soda instead – dipping a damp toothbrush into a pot and then brushing. But if you prefer a thicker, flavoured paste, many green versions of toothpaste now come in a glass jar with a screw top metal lid, such as Georganics Natural Toothpaste.

It may take some time to adjust to a more natural paste because its texture and taste is different from conventional toothpastes. But as many popular brands contain dubious chemicals such as triclosan and harsh abrasives such as silica, your mouth will soon thank you for making the switch.

#76
DON'T NECESSARILY SHUN FLUORIDE

Contrary to what many people believe, fluoride *is* a natural mineral and can be found throughout the earth's crust, in rainwater and in plants. More importantly, it's the only ingredient that is scientifically proven to reduce dental cavities. Thankfully it's possible to find some low-waste eco toothpastes that also contain fluoride, so you can still enjoy the added tooth protection it gives. A good example of a waste-free fluoride toothpaste is US brand Tom's of Maine – widely available online.

#77
PULL YOUR WAY TO HEALTHY TEETH

Based on the Indian tradition of "oil pulling", swilling a natural oil – most often coconut or sesame – around the mouth is an increasingly popular alternative to normal brushing, and can be low waste. The theory is that after two minutes swilling around the mouth, all the bacteria around the teeth bind to the oil, which is then spat out.

Some advocates also like to brush their teeth and tongue with a damp toothbrush after swilling, for an extra clean. You can try oil pulling yourself with a tablespoon of standard coconut or sesame oil – or buy a ready mixed oil, which often contains added ingredients such as mint and eucalyptus oils to freshen breath.

#78
A BETTER BRUSH

Dentists advise changing your toothbrush every three months, but if everyone is using a plastic version, the amount of waste this causes is huge. In fact, it's believed that in the UK alone, about 100 million toothbrushes end up in landfill every year. A good-quality, reusable electric toothbrush is kinder to the environment in the long run. But there are also even greener options out there, such as bamboo toothbrushes with natural bristles, which you can compost after use.

#79
FLOSS WITHOUT GUILT

Most dental floss is made from nylon, which can't be recycled and ends up in landfill or polluting the oceans. Eco floss, on the other hand, is made from biodegradable silk or bamboo fibres lubricated with plant wax. The best ones also come packaged in a compostable case or one made from recyclable metal or glass. Try WooBamboo Eco Floss or The White Teeth Box Bamboo Floss.

#80
CARE ABOUT HAIR

Most of us have plastic hair brushes or combs, so when the time comes to replace them, try switching to a wooden or bamboo brush or comb with natural bristles. Some trichologists say these brushes do a better job of pulling oil from the root to tip, reducing greasy roots and naturally conditioning hair, so it could even help you go an extra day without washing.

#81
COTTON BUD CULL

Plastic cotton buds were one of the top 10 items found on UK beaches by litter collection volunteers for the Marine Conservation Society. So ditch them once and for all. A far greener choice is the completely compostable variety you can widely buy now, made just from wood or paper and natural cotton. But since you're trying to streamline your beauty regime and go waste free, you might be better asking yourself if you really need to use them anyway? Instead of buds, clean fingers will often do the job for makeup removal and are certainly the best choice for the environment!

#82
CHOOSE FLANNEL OVER WIPES

Most cleansing wipes are not biodegradable and can take 100 years or more to break down in landfill. You can now buy eco-friendly varieties, but why not reduce your waste imprint further by picking up a batch of organic, natural-cotton flannels to use with face soap or cleanser? They can be rewashed hundreds of times and last up to a decade or more.

Another easy win is to stop buying disposable tissues and plump for old-fashioned cloth handkerchiefs that can be washed in the machine. As well as reducing your paper use, you'll save on the plastic that is often used to package tissues.

#83
SWAP COTTON WOOL FOR SPONGE

Cotton balls and pads can be composted, but they are often packaged in wasteful plastic bags. Skip the plastic packaging and try reusable facial sponges, which can be bought loose in many natural health stores. They're soft, absorbent and can be thrown into the wash between uses.

#84
TOILET TRAINING

Most toilet paper comes wrapped in plastic and isn't made from recycled paper. So one immediate way to save on waste and help the environment is to buy toilet paper made from recycled material and wrapped in compostable paper or cardboard. Buying online or from your health food shop or local bulk buy store is the most economical way to do this. Another alternative popular with many zero-waste advocates is to invest in a separate bidet or bidet hose attachment for your loo. This will direct a jet of water to clean your bottom completely paper-free.

#85
AIM FOR THE MOON

Standard sanitary products are damaging to the environment when flushed down the toilet and can take up to 500 years to breakdown in landfill when tossed in the bin. Plus, they contain plastics and other chemicals that some experts suspect could be harmful to health in the long term.

As most women will use more than 10,000 sanitary products in their lifetime, switching to eco-friendly options is a game-changer when it comes to reducing your waste imprint.

Swap disposable pads and tampons for reusable cloth pads that can be washed in the machine. Or buy a menstrual cup, a small silicone reusable cup worn internally to collect menstrual blood. They have minimal impact on the environment, are long-lasting and money-saving. Newer still are period panties, an ostensibly normal pair of pants to look at, but with a thicker absorbent gusset that allows you to "free bleed" without leaking, and can hold blood up to the equivalent of two tampons. Again, these can simply be washed in the machine each month and reused for several years.

Why saving water in the bathroom is key

Clean, fresh water might seem like a limitless resource but, without increased conservation efforts, predictions suggest the world could literally run out of usable water. Reducing the amount of water you use reduces the energy required to process and deliver it to homes, businesses, farms and communities, which in turn helps to reduce pollution and conserve fuel resources.

If your home is on a water meter, conservation will also save you money. The bathroom typically uses the most water in any house and there are some simple ways you can use less.

- Keep a bucket in the shower and let it fill up while you wash. You can then use this excess water to flush the toilet – toilet flushing is the single biggest use of water in the house, using 18–27 litres (4–6 gallons) a time.

- Simply turning the tap off while brushing your teeth is important too, and something many of us forget to do! It's also good to bear in mind that while a full bath uses up to 200 litres (45 gallons) of water, a 5-minute shower uses only around 20 litres (4.5 gallons). Which means showering daily and bathing only occasionally makes a big difference – as does having a bath only half full rather than right up to the brim.

OTHER GREEN HOME GET-OUTS

Although the kitchen and bathroom are the two main waste-creating areas in any house, that doesn't mean the rest of your home is completely blameless! There are still plenty of ways you can significantly reduce waste created by other rooms in your home.

#86
THINK SECOND-HAND FIRST

Before buying any new piece of furniture, look into second-hand, upcycled or refurbished options. With a bit of research you can often find items that are as good as new and cheaper to boot. Look to pick something up locally and you also get to give something a second lease of life with little additional transport impact, no packaging and overall lower environmental cost. Besides, a lot of modern furniture isn't built to last and end ups broken and in landfill a few years after it's purchased, especially if you have a young family.

Look on your local community websites and Facebook "buy and sell" pages – you'll be surprised how much good stuff you'll find for or next to nothing or even free.

#87
MAKE CONSCIENTIOUS CHOICES ON NEW

Wherever possible choose items made from glass, metal or sustainable wood, all of which are recyclable. Avoid plastic furniture, as it's rarely able to be recycled and will only end up in landfill.

Watch out for the polyester or acrylic upholstery often used on chairs and lamp shades, which is also non-recyclable. And try to limit the packaging often used to wrap furniture. If an item is being delivered, you might not have a choice, but if you look locally and offer to take it home yourself, you can say no to more packaging and also ask the shop to recycle any excess plastic or cardboard for you. Many businesses now have responsible waste programmes in place – ask in a shop before buying and hand over cash only if you're satisfied with their answer.

#88
BUY A BETTER BED

Invest in the sturdiest wooden or metal-framed bed you can afford, and it will last you many years. When it comes to a new mattress, the better the quality, the longer it will last, which is important because mattresses are one of the hardest items to dispose of in a green way. Ask exactly what the mattress you're buying is made from too, and stick to ones containing sustainable rubber or cotton. The more we ask these kinds of questions before we buy, the more manufacturers will become aware of the high demand for low-waste, greener goods.

#89
PICK SOFT FURNISHINGS MADE FROM NATURAL FABRIC

When it comes to curtains or drapes, towels, bed linen, cushions and rugs, aim for sustainable natural fibres such as cotton, wool and silk. Avoid synthetic microfibres such as polyester, which contain tiny plastic particles that are released into the environment when washed. But do your research first, as some cotton-farming practices use an excessive amount of water, and choose brands that have the most ethical farming credentials.

Wool is increasingly being used in bedding such as duvets and pillowcases and has great warming and cooling properties, which make it well worth the investment. Meanwhile, other sustainable fibres such as organic bamboo have become popular alternatives to cotton bed linen. Where possible, look for items coloured with eco-friendly dyes.

#90
GET HANDY

We live in such a throwaway culture that as soon as something breaks we tend to bin it and go shopping for a replacement. Instead, brush up on your DIY skills. See if you can mend an item, sew up that hole, replace lost screws or repaint that table. Do whatever you can do to patch it up and keep using it. You'll save money, plus it's incredibly satisfying knowing that you're giving an item a longer life.

#91
HAVE A LIGHTBULB MOMENT

Change bulbs to LEDs or invest in other good-quality, energy-efficient light bulbs wherever possible; not only will you have to replace them less often (hence creating less waste in packaging and glass), but they also tend to use up to 75 per cent less energy than traditional incandescent bulbs and can last 25 times longer.

While you're at it, start buying rechargeable batteries instead of disposables – it takes 50 times more energy to make a disposable battery than it provides during its short life, and every year more than 20,000 tonnes (19,700 tons) of batteries are sent to landfill sites in the UK.

#92
BE MORE ENERGY-CONSCIOUS ALL ROUND

Homes are responsible for 14 per cent of greenhouse gas emissions in the UK, so implementing energy efficiency measures in your house can significantly reduce your carbon footprint. Increased energy efficiency will also save you money on bills.

Try the following energy-savings tricks

- Run a dishwasher or washing machine only when it is full.

- Unplug electronics when they're not in use so they don't drain power, or use an electric multipoint power strip, which you can turn off at night.

- Put on an extra jumper before turning up the heating.

- Turn your thermostat as low as you are comfortable with in the winter.

Paper principles

The average UK family throws six trees of paper into their household bin a year, which makes mindful paper use a key area to reduce your waste footprint.

- If you have a home printer, print only if absolutely necessary. If you do, try to fit in as much content into as few pages as possible, and pick sustainable paper made from 100 per cent recycled materials.

- Make digital notes and "to do" lists on your phone or laptop instead of on paper.

- Switch to paperless bills and receipts – this will not only save paper, it will keep your documents more secure, as when you're finished with them, you can just delete the files.

- Say no to junk mail – taking a few minutes to cancel subscriptions and stop any unsolicited junk mail is as simple as going online and clicking a few times to remove yourself from mailing lists. This alone can cut by up to 20 per cent the paper waste you indirectly create.

- Reuse paper – think twice before throwing any paper item away because much of it can be repurposed. Envelopes make great scrap paper, while cardboard, old newspaper and egg boxes can be used by your own kids or donated to local schools for arts and crafts materials. Plus, sheets of newspaper are useful for cleaning greasy pans and barbeques or as a handy alternative to kitchen roll for cleaning windows.

#93
DON'T BUY PLASTIC PENS

A thorough search of your home will probably turn up lots of pens. But if you do have to buy one, choose something that is good quality, long-lasting and a pleasure to write with, such as an old-fashioned fountain pen. When it comes to highlighters, switch to coloured pencils. Not only are they made from wood rather than plastic, with careful sharpening they last significantly longer – saving you money in the long run.

#94
ECO
GIFTING

Gift-giving doesn't have to compromise your zero-waste goals – it just means thinking more creatively. Try making homemade gifts to give to friends and family such as jam, cookies or bath salts. Or choose experience-based gifts rather than material items – for example, a lovely meal out, tickets to the theatre or a pampering spa day.

When it comes to wrapping gifts, most wrapping paper, ribbons and gift tags have a laminated plastic coating, which can't be recycled – not to mention the plastic packaging the wrapping tends to come in. Then there's the unrecyclable sticky tape. Instead, use recycled brown packing paper or old newspaper. Both can look really smart when tied with a colourful cotton ribbon, raffia or simple brown string. You can also use tissue paper, fabric offcuts or leftover wallpaper to make unique, personalized wrapping paper.

BE A WARDROBE WARRIOR

Our ongoing love affair with cheap, fast fashion is nothing short of disastrous for our planet – not to mention the poorly paid workers in developing countries who are often exploited to produce them. The synthetic materials used to make the standard fabrics, such as polyester and nylon, also cause huge pollution during production – then continue to pollute when you get them home. Tiny plastic microfibres wash out of the clothes and make their way into the ocean, where they damage marine life.

#95
JUST BUY LESS

Excess clothes and shoes will eventually become clutter and go out with the rubbish. In fact, 295,000 tons (330,000 US tons) of discarded textiles will either end up in a landfill or be incinerated – neither of which are good for the planet. That old saying "less is more" can really benefit you when it comes to clothes shopping. Ask yourself if you really need something before making every purchase, and always check if you can buy second-hand instead. You will end up with far less clutter and more money to spend on life-affirming experiences rather than things.

#96
DON'T MOOD SHOP

Instead of buying something when you're having a bad day, do something more impactful and nourishing for the soul. Go for a walk, hit the gym, practise yoga, or meet up with a good friend for a natter and a giggle. The mood lift of real tangible experiences has been proven to outlast the temporary "retail high" that so often gets shoppers hooked.

#97
BUY BETTER

Investing in fewer, better-quality clothes is another useful way to reduce excess waste. Not least because high-quality fabrics tend to use natural fibres such as cotton or wool rather than synthetics, which means they last for longer and are easier to recycle. Cheaper garments, meanwhile, are more likely to end up in the charity shop at best or at worst as landfill.

Some synthetic fabrics are recyclable, but it tends to be an expensive process even if your can find a recycling point. Before you commit to your next fashion purchase, it is a good idea to ask yourself: Will I still want to wear this in two years? Will it last that long? How about five or even ten? If the answer is no, then put it back on the shelf and pick something with more longevity.

Five other ways to reduce fashion waste

1. Turn old cotton shirts or towels into handkerchiefs, napkins and cloth bags to store bread and vegetables.

2. Wash your clothes only when they're actually dirty instead of after one wear, and wash them at the coolest possible temperature to get them clean. This will help them last longer.

3. Find a good local cobbler to repair worn-out shoes – as well as reheeling, giving a favourite but battered pair a new inner and outer sole will give you years more wear.

4. Learn how to replace a button, sew up holes or hem skirts and trousers to extend the life of your clothing – or find a good local tailor to help with clothing repairs.

5. Swap, don't shop! Host a regular clothing swap with friends. It's fun, reduces waste and will ensure everyone gets something "new" without spending a penny.

How to have a waste-free wedding

The average wedding now costs an average annual salary – and as you can imagine, all the food, travel and general excess that entails also creates a huge amount of waste. But your Big Day doesn't have to come with a big carbon footprint. Follow the advice below to say "I do" to a low-waste wedding.

The dress
Instead of buying a new wedding gown, hunt through charity and vintage clothing shops for a good second-hand dress. If the fit or look isn't quite right, enlist a local tailor or friend with a talent for sewing, and alter or even upcycle your frock into a bespoke creation.

The guest list
The more people you invite, the bigger the eco footprint and waste accumulation. Instead, why not consider something smaller, more intimate and meaningful, with only your very nearest and dearest there?

The invites
Going paper-free and sending electronic invitations will not only cut waste, it will make the admin side of things a lot easier. Try Paperless Post or Paperless Wedding for simple solutions. If you're determined to send physical invitations, try using recycled paper that can be easily recycled again, which means no foil or glitter! You can even buy recycled wildflower seed paper in specialist shops, which can be planted and grown into beautiful flowers.

The cake

Make the cake yourself for the ultimate low-waste option, or get a "star baker" friend to help you out. Failing that, hunt down a local "naked" bakery that doesn't package its goods in plastic for delivery.

The venue

Replace all plastic straws with cardboard alternatives and hand them out only on request. Ensure all cutlery, plates, napkins and glasses are reusable rather than disposable. And if your venue doesn't have furniture, linens, tableware and cloth napkins, hire them rather than buy new. Think about saving energy too. For example, hosting your event outdoors avoids the need to light a large hall and saves on heating bills. Check the eco sustainability of venues too, as many now use renewable energy sources, such as solar power, which will further reduce your carbon footprint.

The caterers

Pick a company based on their green credentials. Talk to them beforehand about your plans to reduce rubbish and see how they can accommodate. Pick your menu carefully, and ask that it's based on locally sourced produce only. For example, implement a 160-km (100-mile) rule to make sure your food won't create carbon emissions through long-distance travel. Check also that your caterer will be composting food scraps and avoiding cling film (Saran wrap), and find out if they work with any local charities that collect food waste.

The photographer

Choose someone who runs their photography business as greenly as possible. Use digital photography instead of old-fashioned film and consider an online-only photo gallery over endless paper prints and albums. There's no rule that says you need to hire a professional photographer for your wedding either – you could just as easily rely on capable friends and family to take candid, informal photos and video of your day.

The favours

Hand out sustainable gifts such as food treats or potted plants, which won't end up in a landfill where they contribute to global warming. Other ideas include home-made bird feeders, hand-baked confectionary or handmade soap.

The confetti

Provide confetti ready for guests and go for old-fashioned rice or natural flower petals rather than coloured paper or plastic (which are actually banned in an increasing number of places).

RESPONSIBLE RECYCLING

Many people still assume that better recycling is the answer when it comes to dealing with all the billions of tonnes of excess waste we produce. But sadly this isn't the case. The truth is, even if every country, every company and every individual recycled everything they used, it wouldn't be enough to tackle the problems of pollution and climate change. The world today just consumes too much stuff on a daily basis to physically process. And recycling itself also uses huge amounts of resources and energy.

Plus, many items, including plastic, are downcycled rather than recycled, meaning they become an inferior product of lesser quality. After a few more downcycles – or in some cases just one – these products inevitably end up in landfill.

So recycling shouldn't be our first line of defence in going waste free – it should be the last resort.

Yes, we do want to recycle everything we can, but it must come after all other measures have been taken – namely waste prevention, product redesign and changed personal habits.

Take bottled water, for example. Even if we recycled 100 per cent of our plastic water bottles, tap water still uses far fewer resources and produces far fewer greenhouse gas emissions than either the production or recycling of plastic bottles, so is clearly the better environmental choice.

A zero-waste approach evaluates a product's entire lifecycle, not just if it can be recycled or composted. Moving towards a true waste free lifestyle is about recycling less – not more – but knowing how to recycle responsibly is still an important first step. Here are a few tips to improve your recycling game.

#98
GET RECYCLING SAVVY

Research your local council's recycling policies and locations –
are you doing enough to take advantage of them? Could you be
recycling any more of your old food, packaging or garden waste?

   Different areas have different rules when it comes to what can and
can't be recycled, so check with your local authority to find out what
you can recycle via home collection, drop off point or tip.

Two key areas to note

● Plastic: some experts now believe that the biggest
problem with plastic use is not just the sheer scale of it, but
how little attention is paid to finding ways to recycle the
substance in all its forms. As a result only nine per cent of
plastic is currently recycled.

● Electronics: When a computer or mobile phone has
come to the end of its life, be sure to take it to a place that
can either refurbish and resell, or recycle, its respective parts
properly. PCs, laptops and keyboards aren't just made of
plastic – they contain metals that can be given a whole new
life, including gold and copper. Electronics should never be
simply thrown out in the rubbish to end up buried in landfill.
Look online for your nearest electronic recycling centre.

#99
DEVELOP THE HABITS OF A RECYCLER

For example, most jars and yoghurt pots need a clean before they can be recycled, so get used to leaving them to soak in the sink when they're finished – or putting them through the dishwasher with the rest of your wash. Store your food waste container next to the sink and keep your recycling bin next to the main bin so you can take out the rubbish and recycling at the same time each week.

How many times can things be recycled?

Some materials can be recycled again and again, but most can be recycled only a certain number of times before they have to go to landfill. Recycling them should only be a last option when all other forms of reuse have been exhausted...

Plastic: 1–2 times
Most plastics can only be recycled once or twice before they are "downcycled", which means recycled into something of lesser value.

For example, water bottles are often downcycled into fabric or plastic lumber – a type of material that can be used to make garden furniture. But these items can't then be recycled again. So once the fleece jumper or bench is no longer wanted, it just ends up in landfill, where it will sit for thousands of years.

The type of plastics that can be recycled more than once are considered "durable plastics", such as bottle caps. But even bottle caps can only be truly recycled once – after that it has to be downcycled into a non-recyclable material.

Paper: 5–7 times

Believe it or not, paper can be almost as tricky as plastic to recycle, as its recycling potential is lowered after every reuse. This is because paper is made up of long fibres that become shortened every time it's recycled, making it harder to be recycled the next time. For example, the average number of times your printer paper can be recycled is about five to seven times. After that the fibres become too short and can't be made into good-quality paper anymore. From this point, it can be made into more of a paper paste, which is used for items such as newspaper or egg cartons.

Metals and glass: infinitely

All metals have an unlimited lifespan, which is why it's always a good idea to recycle them, regardless of how much you have. Glass, like metal, can be recycled an unlimited number of times, so you should never feel guilty about buying glass as long as you recycle it when you no longer need it. And because glass is harder to create from scratch, it's actually more cost-effective to recycle it than produce it, costing a third less!

#100
MAKE THESE CHANGES FOR LIFE

Now you've worked your way towards a no-waste existence, it's important you turn this transition into permanent change – and don't slip back into any previous wasteful habits.

Hopefully the little changes you've made with the help of this book will have reshaped your entire outlook on how to live your life and care more for the environment.

Waste isn't just physical, it's psychological too – think about how much money, energy and guilt you've saved, and how good that feels. Use these positive vibes as fuel to maintain or even extend your low-waste lifestyle choices.

And remember, as a good citizen you're doing your small but vital bit in a global effort to counter an immediate and deadly threat to our planet.

INDEX

RESOURCES

Further reading:

How to Go Plastic Free, Caroline Jones
How to Go Meat Free, Stepfanie Romine
Zero Waste Home, Bea Johnson
Silo: the Zero Waste Blueprint, Douglas McMaster
The Uninhabitable Earth, David Wallace-Wells

Online:

www.comptoir-des-savonniers-paris.fr
www.ecocycle.org
ethicalsuperstore.com
www.floraandfauna.com.au
www.goingzerowaste.com
halo.coffee
www.harmlessstore.co.uk
www.lesswaste.org.uk
www.litterless.com
www.lovefoodhatewaste.com
www.moncharbon.com
packagefreeshop.com
www.paris-to-go.com
www.planetorganic.com
www.therogueginger.com
www.thecleankilo.co.uk
wildminimalist.com

MAR 1 2 2021